BASKETBALL CHALLENGE

BASKETBALL CHALLENGE

KATHY VANDERLINDEN

GREYSTONE BOOKS

Douglas & McIntyre Publishing Group
Vancouver/Toronto/New York

Copyright © 2000 by Kathy Vanderlinden
00 01 02 03 04   5 4 3 2 1

Greystone Books
A division of Douglas & McIntyre Ltd.
2323 Quebec Street, Suite 201
Vancouver, British Columbia
V5T 4S7

Canadian Cataloguing in Publication Data

Vanderlinden, Kathy.
 Basketball challenge

ISBN 1-55054-753-4

1. Basketball–Miscellanea–Juvenile literature. 2. National
Basketball Association–Miscellanea–Juvenile literature. I. Title.
GV885.1.V36 2000   j796.323   C00-910429-1

Library of Congress Cataloguing-in-Publication Data available upon request.

Editing by Lucy Kenward
Front cover photograph by CP Picture Archive (Kevin Frayer)
Text illustrations by Mark Thurman
Text design by Rose Cowles
Cover design by Tanya Lloyd
Printed and bound in Canada by Transcontinental Printing
Printed on acid-free paper ∞

Kathy Vanderlinden is a Toronto editor and writer who has written several
books for children. She would like to thank Doug Nicholson and Kerry Banks
for sharing their hoops expertise, Lucy Kenward for editing wisely and well.

We gratefully acknowledge the financial support of the Canada Council for the
Arts, the British Columbia Ministry of Tourism, Small Business and Culture,
and the Government of Canada through the Book Publishing Industry
Development Program (BPIDP) for our publishing activities.

Contents

Introduction

Maybe you think of basketball as a game you or your friends play at school and the pros play in the National Basketball Association (NBA). But did you know that more than 300 million people all over the world play the game regularly? And that there are professional leagues not only in North America but also in Europe, Asia, and South America? In fact, basketball is edging out soccer as the world's No. 1 sport.

It's not surprising. Basketball at its best is a spectacular show of speed, strength, and skill that inspires great "oooohs" and "aaaahs" from the fans. The team play and the almost unbelievable, gravity-defying slam dunks of the star players are thrilling to watch. Yet it's a game whose basic skills many kids, both boys and girls, can master and enjoy. You can play winter or summer, anywhere there are a few square meters of space and something to nail a basketball hoop to. Just think of all the garages in North America that have nets attached to them. They show how much fun many people have tossing a ball through a hoop.

Whether you're a mean ball handler who can sink a shot from the top of the "key" or just a fan who'd be happy to lick the dust off Vince Carter's shoes, this book will give you something to do between games. All you need is a pencil and some thinking skills. It helps if you're a basketball genius, but you can often score points just by doing some smart figuring. You might even pick up a few hints to help you with your game. So, grab a pencil and get ready to jam.

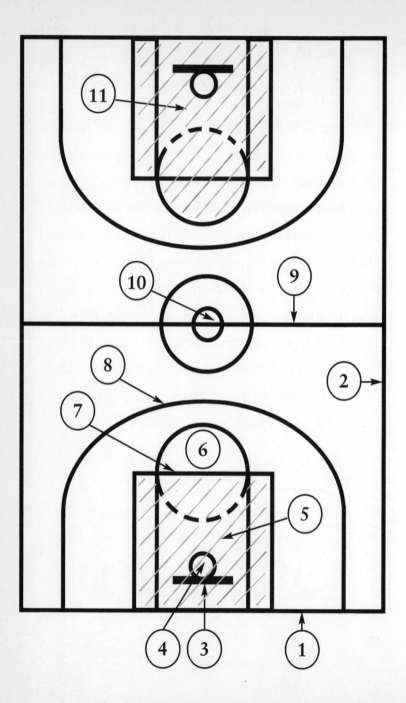

Order in the Court!

A basketball court is a beautiful thing, with its glossy floor and bright colored symbols. And when you know what they mean, you'll have a lot of the game figured out.

So test your knowledge of court proceedings by matching the numbers on the diagram with the correct terms below.

Backboard ___   **Jump-ball circle** ___

Baseline ___   **Key** ___

Basket ___   **Lane** ___

Center court ___   **Sideline** ___

Free-throw line ___   **Three-point line** ___

Half-court line ___

First Shots

Could you invent a game? Dr. James Naismith did, and he called it basketball. He was a Canadian-born teacher at the YMCA International Training School in Springfield, Massachusetts, who created it for his students. On December 21, 1891, they played the world's very first hoops game.

For your first game, check off which of the following descriptions of that match are still true of basketball today.

1. Each team had nine players. ___
2. The goals were two large, round peach baskets. ___
3. The goals were hung at each end of the court 3 meters (10 feet) above the floor. ___
4. The game began with a toss-up at center court. ___
5. Players were not allowed to run carrying the ball. ___
6. It was against the rules to hold, trip, or push an opposing player. ___
7. Players could bat the ball with one or both hands but not hit it with their fists. ___
8. The ball had to stay inside the basket to score. ___
9. If a team made three fouls in a row, the other team was given a goal. ___
10. The winner was the team that made the most baskets in a set time. ___

Move to the Groove

Whether you're a kid shooting hoops in the backyard or a member of an Olympic basketball team, you'll be making many of the same basic moves. (Okay, the Olympic player will probably be making them a bit better.) In this game, decide your moves as you pick the best definition for each of these terms. In some cases, more than one answer is correct.

1. Dribbling

(a) Bouncing the ball with the palm of your hand

(b) Bouncing the ball with your fingers

(c) Not getting the hang of drinking out of a pop can

2. Crossover dribble

(a) Dribbling with one hand crossed over the other

(b) Dribbling from one side of the court to the other

(c) Switching from one hand to the other to change direction

3. **Passing**

(a) Throwing the ball to a teammate

(b) Bouncing the ball to a teammate

(c) Dribbling past a guard

4. **Alley-oop**

(a) A shot made from within the free-throw lane

(b) A pass to a teammate near the basket, who catches the ball on a jump and puts it in

(c) A long one-handed pass similar to throwing a baseball

5. **Layup**

(a) A timeout between game periods

(b) A pass to a teammate who then scores

(c) Jumping up and putting the ball into the net, usually by making it roll off the backboard

Position Posers

A team is not just a bunch of players trying to grab the ball and score. Each person plays a position that has certain duties. Do you know what the players are really doing out there on the court? Fill in the blanks with the correct choices below. (In some cases, more than one answer is correct.)

1. The five player positions are point guard, shooting guard, small forward, power forward, and

    _____.

(a) Center

(b) Shooting forward

(c) Big forward

2. The point guard is also called a

    _____.

(a) "Three"

(b) "One"

(c) Lead guard

3. A point guard should be an excellent
    _____.

(a) Dribbler

(b) Passer

(c) Director

4. Small forwards are called that because
    _____.

(a) They should be quite small.

(b) They are not as big as the power forwards.

(c) They were named after a famous forward of the
    1950s named Otis Small.

5. A_____should be tall, strong, and
    good at defending and rebounding.

(a) Small forward

(b) Shooting guard

(c) Power forward

6. A _____or "five" should be strong
    in both offense and defense.

(a) Center

(b) Shooting guard

(c) Power forward

Talking Pictures

Hot hand, shake and bake, one-three-one—here's a game that'll tone up your talk. Choose the basketball term that best describes what's going on in each of these pictures.

1. (a) Air ball
   (b) Hole-in-one
   (c) Swish

2. (a) Screen
   (b) Open man
   (c) Pine brothers

3. (a) Driving
   (b) Charging
   (c) Traveling

4. (a) Rattler
   (b) Spike
   (c) Shovel

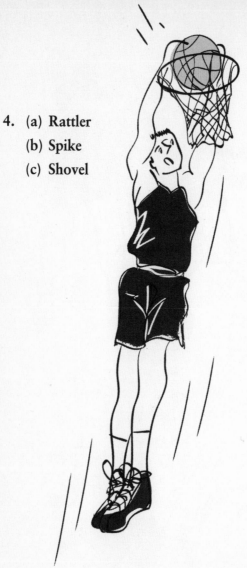

5. (a) Hook
   (b) Kill the clock
   (c) Pump fake

6. (a) Chucker
   (b) Cornrows
   (c) Dipsy-doo

Rules Rock

As basketball has become more complex, so have the rules. For this game, you don't need to be Ruler of the Rules, but it helps if you know you can't use a step-ladder to make a dunk. (It also helps if you know what a dunk is.) Mark these true or false.

1. In women's basketball, the ball is a little smaller than the one used in the men's game. _____

2. When a ball is falling down toward the basket, it's okay for opposing players to hit it out of the way. _____

3. Players cannot run outside the court area and back in again. _____

4. In the opening jump ball, the player who gets the ball should start dribbling right away. _____

5. Players awarded a free throw can take as long as they like before shooting. _____

6. Kicking the ball to a teammate is okay in certain situations. _____

7. A player is allowed to take no more than two steps with the ball before dribbling or passing it.

_____

8. It is against the rules for a player to shoot with his or her back to the basket. _____

9. When guarding a player with the ball, it's okay to force the ball out of his or her hands. _____

10. If a shot misses the basket and bounces off the rim, a teammate can try to grab it and toss it in.

_____

Nicknames Make 'em Friends

Why are basketball stars so often given nicknames? They range from the predictable ("Dollar" Bill Bradley, "Shaq" O'Neal) to the wild and woolly (Jerry "Zeke from Cabin Creek" West, Darrel "Dr. Dunkenstein" Griffith, Kevin "the Black Hole" McHale). Maybe these tags let us feel closer to all that talent, shine, and glory.

Box Scores

Terms, teams, and players are mixed up in this crossword. Figure out the words from the clues and then write them in the diagram.

Across

3. It's made of net: __ __ __ __ __ __.
7. Stuff the ball into the net from above: __ __ __ __.
8. All players __ __ __ to score.
10. Guards try to __ __ __ __ __ the other team's shots.
12. The low __ __ __ __ area is under or near the basket.
14. Another name for a pass: __ __ __ __.
15. "Hi __ __ , it's off to the game we go!"
16. It's against the rules to taunt __ __ yell at a referee.
17. The Los Angeles Lakers' giant, __ __ __ __ O'Neal.
19. Keep your eye __ __ the ball.
20. To pivot, keep one __ __ __ __ on the floor and spin around.
22. A long-distance shot: __ __ __ __.
24. Shooting from "Death Valley" is taking a big __ __ __ __.
25. An official may __ __ __ __ a technical foul.

Down

1. Players may __ __ __ for a timeout.
2. Toss the ball through the __ __ __.
3. The Chicago __ __ __ __ __ __ were the major NBA champs of the 1990s.
4. __ __ air ball misses the basket entirely.
5. Two players guarding one opponent in a corner is a __ __ __ __.

6. The __ __ __ __ __ __ Celtics have won more NBA championships than any other team.

9. Kareem Abdul-Jabbar was a master of the
   __ __ __-__ __ __ __ .

10. 1992 Olympic "Dream Team" member Larry
    __ __ __ __ .

11. __ __ no! He missed!

13. You need to take a __ __ __ __ to score.

14. That team knows what to __ __ to win.

17. You can hear the __ __ __ __ when our team loses!

18. Need cash to buy tickets? Stop at an __ __ __.

21. Repeat of 16 Across.

23. The Grizzlies' home province: __.__.

Fan Protectors

Backboards were put up
behind baskets in 1893
because fans kept interfering
with the ball. The first "boards" were
made of wire, then wood and finally, in
the 1940s, transparent material with
a white rectangle painted on them
for better aiming.

Faking It

You'll probably agree that basketball at its greatest is played by the pro teams of the National Basketball Association (NBA). That's where you'll find the biggest stars and the hottest action. So, slam fans, how well do you know your teams?

1. Here is a list of cities and their teams, only they're not quite right. Write the real names on the lines.

(a) Orlando *Hocus-pocus* _____

(b) Chicago *Cows* _____

(c) Toronto *Dinosaurs* _____

(d) Utah *Rock 'n' Roll* _____

(e) Los Angeles *Rivers* _____

(f) Phoenix *Moons* _____

(g) Sacramento *Princes* _____

(h) Philadelphia *67ers* _____

2. Now try your hand at pictures. Figure out which professional team crests these drawings represent and write the teams' names underneath. (If they look a little weird, it's because details have been changed to make the game more of a challenge.)

(a) —————————

(b) —————————

(c) —————————

(d) —————————

(e) —————————

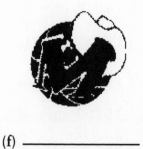

(f) —————————

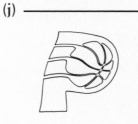

(g) ——————————   (h) ——————————

(i) ——————————   (j) ——————————

(k) ——————————   (l) ——————————

Milwaukee Bucks   Miami Heat

Chicago Bulls   Dallas Mavericks

Cleveland Cavaliers   Indiana Pacers

Boston Celtics   Detroit Pistons

Vancouver Grizzlies   Toronto Raptors

Atlanta Hawks   Minnesota Timberwolves

Rebound Rap

Hey, guy and girlie, here's an ocean of a notion—
Basketball heroes are poetry in motion.
So sharpen up your skills, be a rhymin' machine,
Find the names of these stars of the basketball scene.

First names or last names or full names they could be,
But they rhyme with the italicized phrases that you see.
Here's a hint how it works: "Who's the famous and
adored one?"
Well, the answer's gotta be—former "Air"man Michael
Jordan!

1. He can drive, he can fake, he's sensational at *dunkin'*,
   In fact he does it all, star power forward Tim
   _____.

2. In 1999, do you know what this guy did?
   He got seven triple-doubles, Phoenix point guard
   Jason _____.

3. The coach said that there was no way he'd trade, sell or *barter*

   His main man, his shooting star, Toronto's pride, Vince _____!

4. The Jazz man, the "Mailman," how high that kid has *grown,*

   A super power forward, yeah, it must be Karl

   _____ .

5. Look who nailed a basket with an oh-so-*naughty tip-in—*

   It has to be that mighty man, small forward

   _____ _____.

6. The cows were all out dancing, it was such a *merry herd,*

   "Sure, but can they dipsy-do?" said legendary

   _____ _____.

7. When I'm cooking french fries, I don't give *any lard away,*

   Unless I'm asked politely by the Suns'

   _____ _____.

8. I thought I was in heaven, and I said, "Is this *a Dream?"*

   'Cause I was shooting baskets with that superstar

   _____ .

Renegade!

Meet Disaster Dan—this guy's breaking nearly every rule in the book. Can you spot at least 10 things Dan is doing wrong that could earn him a penalty?

1. _____

2. _____

3. _____

4. _____

5. _____

6. _____

7. _____

8. _____

9. _____

10. _____

HoopSpeak

Here are more words and phrases to show you know your way around a basketball court. Pick the best definition for each. Watch out for steals, fakes, and other sneaky tricks!

1. **Dream Team**
(a) Players on the bench
(b) U.S. All-Star team that won gold at the 1992 Barcelona Olympics
(c) Michael Jordan, Larry Bird, and Magic Johnson
(d) U.S. All-Star winning team at the 1994 World Championship of Basketball in Toronto

2. **Dish**
(a) The basket
(b) A good-looking player
(c) Gossip about players behind their backs
(d) To pass the ball

3. **Flagrant foul**

(a) Swearing at an opponent

(b) Unnecessary and excessive contact with an opponent

(c) When the ball goes out of bounds

(d) A shot so bad it stinks

4. **Double team**

(a) A second team waiting on the bench

(b) Two forwards making a play

(c) Two defense players guarding one opponent

(d) A second team that plays out-of-town games

5. **Field goal**

(a) A basket made from beyond the three-point line

(b) A dunk

(c) A layup

(d) A basket made from within the three-point line

6. **Downtown**

(a) The area behind the net and backboard

(b) The area beyond the three-point line

(c) The heavy action in front of the basket

(d) The bench

Game Time

For a fast-paced game, you need time limits. These statements are all about timing. Mark them true or false. You could even set yourself a time limit to finish—10 minutes should do it.

1. A game has two halves, each 45 minutes long.
   _____

2. There is a 15-minute break between halves. _____

3. Each team gets several brief timeouts per game.
   _____

4. The clock that keeps track of playing time is called the game clock. _____

5. A separate clock, called the shot clock, keeps track of shooting time. _____

6. A team that gets possession of the ball has 30 seconds to take a shot. _____

7. If the team with the ball doesn't take a shot within the time limit, the other team gets a free throw.
   _____

8. A player has five minutes to make a free throw.
   _____

9. At the end of all timeouts, play starts with a jump ball at the center circle. _____

10. If the score is tied at the end of regulation time, the game goes into overtime. _____

11. Overtime continues until one team scores. _____

12. If a player takes a shot and the end-of-period buzzer sounds while the ball is in the air, the goal counts. _____

Record Hogs

Many of the major NBA scoring records are held by two men: Kareem Abdul-Jabbar, who played in the 1970s and '80s, and Wilt Chamberlain, who dominated the 1960s. Chamberlain is still the only player to have scored 100 points in a single game.

Circle Game

At least 26 hoop terms, teams, or players are hidden in this jumble. They can read in any direction—horizontally, vertically, diagonally, backwards, or upside down. And words can overlap, so you'll use some letters more than once. Figure out the words from the clues and then find and circle them in the puzzle. (Hint: The answers to the clues are in alphabetical order.)

```
L  H  E  A  T  K  E  Y  P  L
G  U  A  R  D  O  B  I  I  A
G  I  B  B  L  O  C  K  T  Y
T  N  I  A  P  H  O  O  P  U
O  E  E  L  S  Y  M  L  A  P
H  T  A  L  A  K  E  R  S  M
S  Y  A  O  J  S  E  T  S  U
B  M  O  B  R  I  M  T  M  J
```

Clues

1. That round thing you shoot with: __ __ __ __.

2. The center is usually a __ __ __ , tall player.

3. A guard's aim is to __ __ __ __ __ the shot.

4. A shot made from a long distance: __ __ __ __.

5. The __ __ __ __ is the Miami team.

6. What you throw word No. 1 through: __ __ __ __.

7. The game starts with a __ __ __ __ ball.

8. The lane and free-throw circle in front of the net:

   __ __ __.

9. Kobe Bryant plays for the Los Angeles __ __ __ __ __ __.

10. A close-to-the-net shot usually bounced off the

    backboard: __ __ __ __ __.

11. A soft, high-arcing shot or pass: __ __ __.

12. One of Michael Jordan's nicknames: __ __.

13. You throw word No. 1 through this, too: __ __ __.

14. The free-throw lane is also called "the

    __ __ __ __ __."

15. It's a violation to scoop, or __ __ __ __, the ball

    while dribbling.

16. A good player learns to __ __ __ __ as well as shoot.

17. The pick-and-roll is a useful offensive __ __ __ __.

18. A missed shot can bounce off the basket __ __ __.

19. To make a __ __ __ shot you push with your legs

    but don't jump.

20. The layup is a basic __ __ __ __.

21. A long arcing shot so high it seems to drop from the sky: __ __ __-__ __ __ __.
22. A forceful dunk: __ __ __ __.
23. A clever move to snatch the ball from an opponent:

__ __ __ __ __.
24. Players have __ __ __ seconds to make a free throw.
25. An even score is a __ __ __.
26. If the ball hits the rim, a player can try for a

__ __ __-in.

Rehearsing for His Role?

Back in 1946, Chuck Connors, playing for the Boston Celtics, grabbed the basket rim going in for a layup and shattered the glass backboard. It was the first, but not the last, time a board's been broken in a hoops game. Connors went on to star in a popular 1950s TV series, *The Rifleman*.

Game of the Names

Did you ever wonder where pro teams get their names?
Most of them suggest strength and energy, and even a
killer instinct—the better to pulverize the competition.
Do you know the name of the following teams?

1. List two team names that are flying creatures.

   _____

2. List three teams named after animals.

   _____

3. List two team names that suggest heat.

   _____

4. Which team name is a kind of music?

   _____

5. Name two women's professional teams.

   _____

6. Which name sounds like a body of water?

   _____

Foul Play

Basketball has rules that define everything about the game—how the court is laid out, what equipment to use, how to play the game, and how to behave while playing it. Breaking a rule is a violation or a foul and may call for a penalty. Check off which of the following are *against* the rules.

1. Hanging on the basket rim to avoid getting hurt

   _____

2. Having seven team members on the court at once

   _____

3. Wearing shorts that end just above the knee _____

4. Arguing with the referee about a bad decision

   _____

5. Running then sliding along the floor to gain ground _____

6. Punching an opponent who has been playing rough _____

7. Dribbling with one hand and then changing to the other _____

8. Stopping a dribble, taking a step, then dribbling again _____

9. Wearing knee guards _____

10. Standing between a team member and his or her guard _____

11. Faking a free-throw attempt _____

12. Grabbing a player's arm to stop his or her progress _____

13. Grabbing the ball in mid-air when an opposing player takes a shot _____

14. Waving your arms to distract a player attempting a free throw _____

15. Flicking the ball out of a dribbler's hand _____

Amazing Feats

Shaquille O'Neal and Dikembe Mutombo have the biggest feet in pro basketball—they wear size 22 shoes.

Three-Point Lines

The three items in each of these groups have something in common. Pick what it is from the answers below.

1. **Leslie, Lobo, Swoopes**
(a) First three women signed to play on the Women's National Basketball Association (WNBA) team
(b) Champion NBA rebounders
(c) Basketball stadiums

2. **Downtown, lane, key**
(a) Places where games can be played
(b) Names for the free-throw line
(c) Parts of a basketball court

3. **Hornets, Bulls, Hawks**
(a) Animals
(b) Men's basketball teams
(c) Women's basketball teams

4. **Backdoor, steal, travel**

(a) Hoops terms

(b) Game violations

(c) Plan for a robbery

5. **Heat, Jazz, Magic**

(a) Great things

(b) Great teams

(c) Great players' nicknames

6. **Allen Iverson, Tim Duncan, Vince Carter**

(a) All play for the Los Angeles Lakers

(b) All are point guards

(c) All won Rookie of the Year awards

Who Dunnit?

How well do you know the pros, both on and off the court? On the lines below, write your picks for who did what. (Hint: All the correct names are in the list, along with a few extras. Some answers may be used more than once. Bonus points for spotting a "double-triple" hidden in this game.)

1. Who appeared in the 1997 movie *Double Team* along with martial arts star Jean-Claude Van Damme? _____

2. Who wrote a book for children called *Shaq and the Beanstalk and Other Very Tall Tales?*

   _____

3. What dynamic New York Knicks shooting guard made a successful comeback in 1999 after a 68-game suspension? _____

4. What Los Angeles Lakers star has released five rap albums? Oh, and he's appeared in five movies, too.

   _____

5. Which Houston Rocket's knee injury in December 1999 ended his NBA career? _____

6. What Chicago Bulls superstar quit to play baseball in 1993, only to return to the courts in 1995?

   _____

7. On January 13, 1999, one of basketball's all-time greatest players retired from the game. Who was he? _____

8. What rebound champ is also famous for wild stunts such as sporting multicolored hair and wearing a wedding dress to public events?

   _____

9. Which legendary star of the 1960s once played for the exhibition team the Harlem Globetrotters?

   _____

10. Which pro player is also a fashion model?

    _____

Charles Barkley

Mike Bibby

Vince Carter

Wilt Chamberlain

Patrick Ewing

Allen Iverson

Michael Jordan

Lisa Leslie

Shaquille O'Neal

David Robinson

Dennis Rodman

Latrell Sprewell

Sheryl Swoopes

Chris Webber

Crossover

Here are some more b-ball words to puzzle over.
Remember, the words have to make sense both down
and across. You know the rules, so follow the clues.

Across

1. In a bank shot, the ball bounces off the
   _ _ _ _ _ _ into the net.
4. When posting up, keep your _ _ _ _ to the
   basket.
6. Every game starts with a _ _ _ _ _ _ _ _ _.
8. If you're doing this puzzle, you're probably a
   basketball _ _ _!
9. The _ _ _ _ game of the series decides the
   winner.
11. Alonzo Mourning's nickname: _ _.
12. An unguarded player: an _ _ _ _ man.
13. "Ho, _ _!" said the guard as he stole the ball
    from the dribbler.
14. After a dribble, players must pass _ _ shoot.

16. An offensive play in which a player stands between a teammate and his or her guard: __ __ __ __ __ __.
18. I've got a __ __ __ __ of tickets to the game for you and me."
22. A pass to a player who scores is an __ __ __ __ __ __ __.
24. Scoring field __ __ __ __ __ is the point of the game.
27. The team that scores the __ __ __ __ points wins the game.
29. A casual game with your friends: pick-__ __.
30. The New Jersey __ __ __ __ __.
32. The __ __ __ __ __ __ part of a basketball is full of air.
34. Those players are as alike as two peas in a __ __ __.

Down

2. Vince Carter plays for the __ __ __ __ __ __ __.
3. Fancy faking by the ball handler: "__ __ __ __ __ and bake."
4. It's round and it's orange: __ __ __ __.
5. An aggressive rebounder will "__ __ __ __ __ the boards."
6. The Utah __ __ __ __ used to be a New Orleans team.
7. Before he retired, Michael Jordan was numero __ __ __ on the Bulls team.
10. __ __ __ __ the ball into the net.

15. After a missed shot, players compete for the

    __ __ __ __ __ __ __.

17. The center __ __ __ __ quickly left to receive the
    pass.

18. The marked-off area in front of the net, up to the
    free-throw line: the " __ __ __ __ __ __."

19. Her jump shot was as smooth __ __ silk.

20. Basketball __ __ beautiful!

21. Shots often bounce off basket __ __ __ __.

23. With 26, a not bad, or __ __-__ __ , game.
    (2 words)

25. Calling the referee a "big, hairy __ __ __" would
    be ruled a technical foul.

26. See 23.

28. When the ball hits the rim, try to __ __ __ it into
    the net.

31. Toronto is often called __. __.

33. __ __ fighting is allowed during a game.

Triple-Doubles

It's quite a feat to make 10 or more points, assists, and rebounds in a single game. That's called a "triple-double"—a double-figure score in any three of these statistical categories: points, assists, rebounds, blocked shots, and steals.

Here is a list of doubles. The trick is to pick what the two items have in common from the triple choice below. (Clue: This game is all about records, record-keeping, and awards.)

1. Michael Jordan and Wilt Chamberlain

(a) They endorsed the same brand of basketball shoes.

(b) They won NBA Rookie of the Year awards.

(c) They own the NBA's two highest points-per-game averages.

2. John Stockton and Magic Johnson

(a) They are the NBA's top two leaders in steals per game.

(b) They are the NBA's top two leaders in total assists.

(c) They played on the same NBA Championship team.

3. **Boston Celtics and Chicago Bulls**

(a) They have met more times in the NBA finals than any other two teams.

(b) They are the only teams to win at least three NBA Championships in a row.

(c) They have never won an NBA Championship.

4. **Nera White and Michael Jordan**

(a) They won several Most Valuable Player (MVP) awards.

(b) They are cousins.

(c) They played on an NBA Championship team in their rookie year as a pro.

5. **Free throws and three–point field goals**

(a) Categories in which Shaquille O'Neal excels.

(b) Categories besides the main five for which statistics are kept.

(c) Categories in which Wilt Chamberlain excelled.

6. **Vince Carter and Michael Jordan**

(a) They both were the first overall picks in the NBA draft.

(b) They both won All-Star Slam Dunk contests.

(c) They both scored 100 points in an NBA game.

Shooting Gallery

For the biggest thrills, nothing beats shooting. Ready to take your shot? Slot the right term from the list below into each blank space. (Careful: There are more terms than blank spaces—and you have to use some terms more than once.)

1. The spectacular _____ is a shot made from the side or backwards, with one hand, in a sweeping arc so high the ball seems to drop from the heavens.

2. When a player is fouled, the referee might award him or her a _____ .

3. Star of the 1980s Kareem Abdul-Jabbar was a master of the _____, which he threw from such a height it was next to impossible to block.

4. Mostly a specialty of very tall players, the _____ is made by jumping high enough to stuff the ball into the net from above.

5. Players get three points if they make a basket from beyond the _____ .

6. For a regular _____ , shooters get two points.

7. A successful free throw is worth _____ point(s).

8. Most players shoot free throws _____ .

9. If player A attempts a free throw and player B tips the ball into the net, _____ gets the point(s).

10. When a shot misses the net and bounces off the backboard, players try for a _____ .

dunk	player A
field goal	player B
free throw	rebound
hook shot	sky-hook
layup	slam
one	three
overhand	three-point line
pass	underhand

Oddballs

In each of these groups, two things are alike and one
thing's a poser. Detect the oddball in each group and
write below why it doesn't fit with the others.

1. (a) **MVP**
   (b) **PPG**
   (c) **DPY**
   (d) **ROY**

   _____

   _____

2. (a) **Zo**
   (b) **White Chocolate**
   (c) **Penny**
   (d) **Loonie**

   _____

   _____

3. (a) **Starzz**
   (b) **Sparks**
   (c) **Suns**
   (d) **Comets**

   _____

   _____

4. (a) **Rock**
   (b) **Pumpkin**
   (c) **Biscuit**
   (d) **Bomb**

   _____

   _____

5. (a) **Team loses possession of the ball**
   (b) **Player has to pay a fine**
   (c) **Player is sprayed with a water hose**
   (d) **Opposing team gets a free throw**

   _____

   _____

Sign Language

Basketball referees call the shots. And they signal their calls with their hands. Do you know what they're saying when they wiggle their fingers and wave their arms? Match the actions on the opposite page to the list of calls below.

Blocking

Holding

Illegal dribbling

Pushing

Technical foul

Three-point field goal attempt

Three-point field goal successful

Traveling

20-second timeout

(b) _____

(a) _____

(c) _____

(e) _____

(d) _____

(f) _____

(h) _____

(g) _____

(i) _____

Play-by-Play

Sportscasters describe games in "hoopese." Explain on the lines following each play what the announcer is talking about. Careful! This reporter has made a foul. Bonus points for catching it.

1. Blue throws up the alley-oop for White.

    _____

    _____

2. Green scoops it off the boards.

    _____

    _____

3. Trailing by one point, the Leopards decide to foul
    the Bears.

    _____

    _____

4. Red drives coast-to-coast.

_____

_____

5. Gray finds the open man for a pass.

_____

_____

6. Navy nets a three-pointer from 5 m (16 ft.) out.

_____

_____

Never Give Up

Michael Jordan, considered by many the greatest basketball player ever, was cut from his second-year high school team. (He made the team the following year.)

All Mixed Up

Here are a bunch of weird sentences that need some help. Each one has a term in italics that makes no sense—at least, not the way it's written. But move the letters around a bit, and you've got a score. Write the correct words on the lines below.

1. The most common hoops shot at the pro level is the *mpuj thso*. _____

2. Pushing, charging, and tripping are examples of *sloapren* fouls. _____

3. During the 1990s, the *oagicch slubl* won six NBA championships. _____

4. Moving the ball from one hand to the other while dribbling is called a *scroosrev* dribble.

   _____

5. When offensive players suddenly move the ball down court at top speed, they're making a *staf krabe*.

   _____

6. Basketball first became an *clyopim* sport at the 1936 Games in Berlin, Germany. _____

7. Every team has a number of *bittessusut* who wait on the bench until called in to replace one of the starting players.

_____

8. From 1959 to 1966, the *soonbt steccil* won every NBA Championship—a record eight in a row.

_____

9. The *accho* is a teacher, organizer, and commander of a team. _____

10. Bumping into an opposing player on purpose would be ruled a *ralftang* foul. _____

Brother and Sister Act

Cheryl Miller and her little brother Reggie have both won Olympic gold as members of U.S. national "Dream Teams"—Cheryl in 1984 at the Los Angeles Olympics and Reggie in Barcelona in 1992.

Girls Got Game

Girls have been playing basketball almost from the time Dr. Naismith invented the game in 1891. Just a year later, Senda Berenson Abbott, an instructor at Smith College in Northampton, Massachusetts, adapted the rules to make the game less rough and more suitable for young ladies. Today, the rules are much the same as for men, and women are tearing up the courts in amateur and professional leagues all over the world.

How much do you know about this fastest-growing area of the hoops scene? Pick the correct endings for each of these statements. (In some questions, more than one answer is correct.)

1. A woman first tried out for an NBA team in:
(a) 1997
(b) 1993
(c) 1979

2. The women's game is played mostly "below the rim." This means:
(a) Close to the basket
(b) Inside the three-point line
(c) With few slam dunks or sky-hooks

3. Compared with the men's game, women players focus more on:
(a) Precision
(b) Smart moves and plays
(c) Avoiding fouls

4. The American Basketball League and the Women's National Basketball Association (WNBA) are:
(a) American women's professional leagues established in 1997
(b) Rival leagues that compete against each other
(c) Leagues that play in the World Championship of Basketball

5. From the 1930s to the 1990s, women's teams generally had:

(a) Five players

(b) 10 players

(c) Six players

6. Before 1997, women could play professionally only in:

(a) Italy

(b) Europe, Asia, and South America

(c) United States

7. The U.S. women's team that won Olympic gold in 1996 included:

(a) Lisa Leslie

(b) Rebecca Lobo

(c) Cheryl Miller

8. At college and pro levels today, women's uniforms, unlike men's:

(a) Have much longer shorts

(b) Can have jerseys worn outside the shorts

(c) Have jerseys with short sleeves

Alphabet Hoop

FTA, PPG, 3PA—game reports and player statistics are full of these puzzling abbreviations. Show your stat savvy by decoding the following letter jumbles.

1. FGA
(a) foul game attempt
(b) field goals attempted
(c) first game assist

2. FGM
(a) field goals made
(b) foul game managed
(c) fine game manners

3. FTA
(a) first team award
(b) first team assist
(c) free throws attempted

4. FTM

(a) free throws made

(b) first team member

(c) fancy tactics move

5. PPG

(a) two-penalty game

(b) points per game

(c) penalties per game

6. PF

(a) player fakes

(b) personal fouls

(c) player fouls

7. OR

(a) overtime rounds

(b) overtime rebounds

(c) offensive rebounds

8. DR

(a) defensive rebounds

(b) drives

(c) dribbles

9. **ST**

(a) statistics

(b) steals

(c) shots taken

10. **BS**

(a) ball steals

(b) blocked shots

(c) bad shots

11. **3P**

(a) three players

(b) three-point shots

(c) three-plays

12. **3PA**

(a) three-point assists

(b) three-point shots attempted

(c) three-play attempts

Word Jam

Here's another scramble of basketball words to find and circle. First solve the clues—the answer words are in alphabetical order. Then find these words in the puzzle.

M	O	R	F	R	B	S	S	U	S
C	I	O	U	I	E	C	P	N	T
T	U	T	I	M	E	O	U	T	E
L	O	S	A	Q	Z	R	R	E	A
H	P	G	M	A	T	E	S	L	L
M	I	C	I	H	E	A	T	Q	A
C	V	U	Q	S	I	X	T	H	O
O	N	T	N	O	T	S	O	B	G

Clues:

1. Grizzlies home town: Vancouver, __.__.
2. The __ __ __ __ __ __ Celtics
3. She made a fast __ __ __ to the left to receive the pass.
4. Illegal contact with an opposing player: __ __ __ __ __
5. He made a nifty steal __ __ __ __ the dribbler.
6. A basket: __ __ __ __
7. "He __ __ __ game!"
8. The Miami __ __ __ __
9. That player's sizzling __ __ __ tonight!
10. The __. __. Lakers
11. The Orlando __ __ __ __ __
12. Players on a team: team__ __ __ __ __
13. __ __ tripping is allowed.
14. The ball balanced __ __ the rim and then fell in.
15. "One more foul and you're __ __ __ of the game!"
16. That basket was a __ __ __ - rattler.
17. In a fast game, you have to be ready to __ __ __.
18. What was the __ __ __ __ __ at half time?
19. Shaquille O'Neal's nickname: __ __ __ __ __
20. Substitute player: __ __ __ __ __ man
21. The San Antonio __ __ __ __ __ __
22. Legally grab the ball from a player: __ __ __ __ __ __
23. __ __ __ Duncan
24. Call for a 20-second __ __ __ __out.

61

Skill Drill

Basketball has four basic skills—shooting, passing, dribbling, and rebounding. Master those and you're on the way to playing a decent game of hoops. Check your fundamentals know-how by marking these statements true or false.

1. Players are either right-handed or left-handed dribblers. _____

2. You should always keep your eye on the ball while dribbling. _____

3. Two basic passes are the chest pass and the bounce pass. _____

4. Another basic pass is the behind-the-back pass.

   _____

5. Most passes should be made with one hand. _____

6. It is a violation to fake a pass. _____

7. If you pass to a teammate who scores, you get one point for the assist. _____

8. The alley-oop pass is one of the easiest to master.

   _____

9. When preparing to shoot, you should hold the ball firmly in the palms of both hands. _____

10. In a bank shot, you aim for the backboard. _____

11. For a hook shot, you start facing the basket. _____

12. A free throw is worth three points. _____

13. A field goal from within the three-point line gets two points. _____

14. A good rebounder should also be a good blocker. _____

15. If you grab a rebound and score, you get one point. _____

Better than the "New York Overalls"

The New York Knickerbockers (or Knicks) probably were named after the city's early Dutch settlers and an old nickname for New Yorkers in general. Knickerbockers are also a style of knee-length, gathered pants—the kind golfers used to wear.

Answers

Game 1
Order in the Court!

Backboard _3_ .

Baseline _1_ . Also called the end line. The two baselines and two sidelines mark off the playing area.

Basket _4_ . The goal.

Center court _10_ . The game begins here with a ball toss for two opposing players to jump for.

Free-throw line _7_ . Free throws, taken from this line, are awarded for fouls (illegal contact) by opposing players.

Half-court line _9_ . Also called the center line or division line, it separates the court into equal halves. Each team defends its half.

Jump-ball circle _6_ . When two opposing players get the ball at the same time, a jump ball may be called at the nearest of these two circles.

Key _11_ . The lane plus the jump-ball circle. Its earlier shape looked like an old-fashioned keyhole.

Lane _5_ . Also called the free-throw lane, the foul lane, or "the paint," this is the painted area in front of each net where most of the action takes place.

Sideline _2_ .

Three-point line _8_ . A basket made from outside this line is worth three points.

Game 2
First Shots

1. No. Today each team has five players. Eighteen men played that first hoops game because that's how many students there were in Naismith's class.

2. Nobody checked this one, we hope. Peach baskets were handy targets for that first game but proved pretty flimsy for regular play. Today's goal is a net attached to a metal hoop.

3. Check. The 3-meter (10-foot) height is still standard. In that first game, it just happened to be the height of the balcony above the gym.

4. Check. Naismith threw a soccer ball up for two players to jump for, and games have started that way ever since. Except now it's a basketball.

5. Check, and you can't walk carrying it, either. Later, dribbling was introduced to allow a player to take the ball down the court.

6. Check.
7. Check. Hitting the ball with your fist is okay in volleyball, but it's not a basketball move.
8. Not any more. At first, basketball nets were closed at the bottom like baskets. But in 1912 the nets were opened, and basketballs have been falling through them ever since.
9. No. Penalties for most fouls now are loss of the ball or a free throw for the other side.
10. Check.

Game 3

Move to the Groove

1. (b) Bouncing the ball with your fingers. Also called ball handling, dribbling is how players move the ball down the court. Great dribbling is one skill that separates the stars from the earthlings.
2. (c) Switching from one hand to the other to change direction. If you're dribbling with your right hand, you bounce the ball across your body to your left hand and continue the dribble from there. A good way to get around a guard.
3. (a) Throwing the ball to a teammate and (b) bouncing the ball to a teammate are both good

ways to pass the ball. A pass gets the ball down court faster than dribbling and is often your best move.

4. (b) A pass to a teammate near the basket, who catches the ball on a jump and puts it in. This one requires perfect timing. (c) is called a baseball pass.

5. (c) Jumping up and laying the ball into the net, usually by making it roll off the backboard. This basic shot is made close to the net and from the side.

Game 4
Position Posers

1. (a) Center.
2. (b) "One" and (c) Lead guard. Each position has a number from one to five.
3. (a) Dribbler, (b) Passer, and (c) Director. The point guard's job is to direct the plays and get the ball up the court.
4. (b) They are not as big as power forwards. It's all relative in basketball, in which height is an asset. As for Otis Small—no such player.
5. (c) Power forward. Sometimes called a "big forward," this player excels at blocking shots.

6. (a) Center. This player is the center of both defensive and offensive action.

Game 5
Talking Pictures

1. (c) Swish. In this shot, the ball goes through the net without touching the rim or backboard. An air ball is a shot so wide of the mark it hits nothing but air. A hole-in-one is a great shot in golf.
2. (a) Screen. Setting a screen (or "pick") means shielding a teammate from his or her guard. An open man is an unguarded player, and pine brothers are substitute players sitting on the bench (pining away?).
3. (a) Driving. Dribbling fast toward the basket. Charging and traveling are violations.
4. (b) Spike. Another name for a dunk (slam or jam), this is basketball's flashiest shot. The player jumps high enough to stuff the ball into the basket from above. A rattler is a shot in which the ball rattles around in the hoop before dropping through the net. A shovel is an underhand shot.
5. (c) Pump fake. A player fakes a move as if to shoot, hoping the guard will jump up. When the guard comes down, the shooter goes up for a real

shot. A hook is a one-handed twisting shot.
To kill the clock means stalling to use up time.

6. (c) Dipsy-doo. This is whizz-bang ball handling
   that fans love to watch. A chucker takes lots of
   shots, and cornrows is a close, braided hairstyle
   sported in the 1999–2000 season by several top
   players such as Latrell Sprewell and Allen Iverson.

Game 6
Rules Rock

1. True. Girls and women play with a ball that's
   about 2.5 cm (1 in.) smaller in circumference and
   a little lighter.
2. False. Opposing players can try to knock the ball
   off course only until it reaches its highest point.
   Once it starts the downward fall, it's hands off.
3. True. Players can go outside the court area only to
   throw in the ball after a goal or violation, or
   when the ball has gone out of bounds.
4. False. Players involved in any jump ball must tap
   the ball to a teammate.
5. False. They have 10 seconds to shoot.
6. False. Kicking the ball is never okay and will
   earn a penalty.

7. False. In some situations players can take one step carrying the ball. Two steps or more is a violation called "traveling."

8. False. Shooting when you can't see the basket might be risky, but it's not against the rules.

9. False. You can't use excessive force to get the ball away from an opponent. You can slap the ball away or grab it while it's in the air.

10. Absolutely. It's called rebounding, and it's one of basketball's basic moves.

Game 7
Box Scores

Game 8
Faking It

1.

(a) Orlando Magic

(b) Chicago Bulls

(c) Toronto Raptors

(d) Utah Jazz

(e) Los Angeles Lakers

(f) Phoenix Suns

(g) Sacramento Kings

(h) Philadelphia 76ers

2.

(a) Atlanta Hawks

(b) Detroit Pistons

(c) Boston Celtics

(d) Milwaukee Bucks

(e) Cleveland Cavaliers

(f) Dallas Mavericks

(g) Toronto Raptors

(h) Miami Heat

(i) Chicago Bulls

(j) Vancouver Grizzlies

(k) Minnesota Timberwolves

(l) Indiana Pacers

Game 9

Rebound Rap

1. Duncan
2. Kidd
3. Carter
4. Malone
5. Scottie Pippen
6. Larry Bird
7. Penny Hardaway
8. Hakeem (Olajuwon), nicknamed "the Dream"

Game 10

Renegade!

Wearing a hat

Wearing jewelry (an earring)

Wearing shirt untucked

Wearing a T-shirt

Wearing shirt with advertising logo

Swearing

Complaining

Elbowing another player

Carrying the ball

Wearing the wrong shoes (these are for football)

Game 11
HoopSpeak

1. (b) U.S. All-Star team that won gold at the 1992 Barcelona Olympics and (d) U.S. All-Star winning team at the 1994 World Championship of Basketball in Toronto. Both were called Dream Teams because they were made up of some of the greatest basketball players of all time. Half points for (c) Michael Jordan, Larry Bird, and Magic Johnson, who were three of the 12 players on the 1992 team.

2. (d) To pass the ball.

3. (b) Unnecessary and excessive contact with an opponent.

4. (c) Two defense players guarding one opponent.

5. All of the above! (a) A basket made from beyond the three-point line, (b) A dunk, (c) A layup, and (d) A basket made from within the three-point line are all examples of field goals, or baskets.

6. (b) The area beyond the three-point line. A field goal from here gets three points.

Game 12
Game Time

1. False. Game length depends on the level of play, but no league has games that long. NBA games are divided into four periods of 12 minutes each; college games have two 20-minute halves.
2. True.
3. True. The number and length of timeouts vary depending on the level of play but are never longer than 100 seconds. They also vary depending on whether or not the game is being shown on TV. In a televised game, several timeouts have to be scheduled for the commercials.
4. True.
5. True. In pro ball, it's also called the 24-second clock; in college games, the 45-second clock.
6. True in women's college games. In pro games, teams have 24 seconds to take a shot, and in college men's games, 45 seconds.
7. False. The opposing team gets possession of the ball.
8. False. Five minutes would be a chess game! Players get 10 seconds to make a free throw.
9. False. Depending on the reason for the timeout, play can start with a jump ball but generally starts with the ball being thrown in from the sidelines.

10. True.

11. False. Overtime periods are 5 minutes long. If the score is still tied, teams play additional 5-minute periods until the score is not tied at the end of a period.

12. True.

Game 13
Circle Game

1. ball
2. big
3. block
4. bomb
5. Heat
6. hoop
7. jump
8. key
9. Lakers
10. layup
11. lob
12. MJ
13. net
14. paint
15. palm
16. pass
17. play
18. rim
19. set
20. shot
21. sky-hook
22. slam
23. steal
24. ten (No. 13 reading up)
25. tie
26. tip

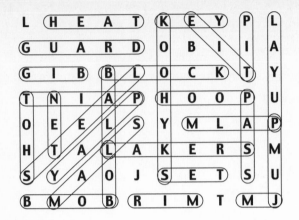

Game 14
Game of the Names

1. Atlanta Hawks, Charlotte Hornets (half points for Houston Rockets, Seattle SuperSonics)
2. Any three of Chicago Bulls, Milwaukee Bucks, Vancouver Grizzlies, Toronto Raptors, Minnesota Timberwolves
3. Miami Heat, Phoenix Suns
4. Utah Jazz
5. Any two of the following: New England Blizzard, Atlanta Glory, San Jose Lasers, Portland Power, Columbus Quest, Richmond Rage, Seattle Reign, Colorado Xplosion (all in the American Basketball League), Houston Comets, New York Liberty,

Phoenix Mercury, Sacramento Monarchs, Cleveland Rockers, Los Angeles Sparks, Utah Starzz, Charlotte Sting (all in the Women's National Basketball Association).

6. Los Angeles Lakers

Game 15
Foul Play

1. No, if done to avoid injury, but otherwise a violation.
2. Check. Only five members are permitted to play at once.
3. No. Long, baggy shorts are having a style moment.
4. Check. If arguing with the referee were permitted, games could get ugly.
5. Check. That would be baseball.
6. Check.
7. No. If you can do this, you're a pretty good ball handler.
8. Check. Once you stop dribbling, you have to pass or shoot.
9. No, as long as they are not made of hard material that could hurt somebody.
10. No. It's called setting a screen.

11. Check. It's fine to fake other shots, though.

12. Check. This is a foul called holding.

13. No, if you can do it! But it would have to be when the ball is heading toward the basket. Once it is on its downward arc into the basket, opposing players must keep hands off.

14. Check. Free throws must be free of distraction too.

15. No. In fact, it's a good move.

Game 16

Three-Point Lines

1. (a) First three women signed to play on the Women's National Basketball Association (WNBA) team. Lisa Leslie, Rebecca Lobo, and Sheryl Swoopes played in the league's first season in the summer of 1997.

2. (c) Parts of a basketball court.

3. (b) Men's basketball teams.

4. (a) Hoops terms. Traveling is a violation, but stealing is perfectly fine.

5. (b) Great teams. Full names are the Miami Heat, Utah Jazz, and Orlando Magic. Magic was the nickname of Earvin "Magic" Johnson, but nobody gets called Heat or Jazz, at least as far as we know.

6. (c) All won Rookie of the Year awards. Allen
Iverson won the award in 1997, Tim Duncan in
1998, and Vince Carter in 1999.

Game 17
Who Dunnit?

1. Dennis Rodman
2. Shaquille O'Neal
3. Latrell Sprewell
4. Shaquille O'Neal
5. Charles Barkley

6. Michael Jordan
7. Michael Jordan
8. Dennis Rodman
9. Wilt Chamberlain
10. Lisa Leslie

The "double-triple" is three names that are the
answers to two questions each: Michael Jordan,
Shaquille O'Neal and Dennis Rodman.

Game 18
Crossover

¹B	O	A	²R	D	³S		⁴B	A	⁵C	K
			A		H		A		R	
	⁶J	⁷U	M	P	B	A	L	L	A	
⁸F	A	N	T		K		⁹L	A	S	¹⁰T
	¹¹Z	O		¹²O	P	E	N		¹³H	O
	Z		¹⁴O	R			¹⁵R			S
				¹⁶S	¹⁷C	R	E	E	N	S
¹⁸P	¹⁹A	²⁰I	²¹R		U		B			
²²A	S	S	I	²³S	T		²⁴G	O	²⁵A	L ²⁶S
I			²⁷M	O	S	²⁸T		²⁹U	P	O
³⁰N	E	³¹T	S			³²I	³³N	N	E	R
T		O				³⁴P	O	D		

Game 19
Triple–Doubles

1. (c) They own the NBA's two highest points-per-game averages. Jordan's average was 31.7 and Chamberlain's 30.1.

2. (b) They are the NBA's top two leaders in total assists. Stockton's career total (up to 1999) is 13,067, and Johnson's is 10,141. John Stockton is also the NBA leader in career steals, and Magic is not far behind—he's No. 9.

3. (b) They are the only teams to win at least three NBA Championships in a row. The Boston Celtics in fact won eight in a row (1959–66). The Chicago Bulls won three in a row twice, from 1991–93 and from 1996–98.

4. (a) Both won several Most Valuable Player (MVP) awards. Nera White, playing on the U.S. national team, won her 11th MVP at the 1957 World Championship of Basketball and was later named the greatest woman player in the world. Jordan won six MVP awards during the 1990s.

5. (b) Categories besides the main five for which statistics are kept. O'Neal and Chamberlain, despite their many other achievements, have sunk only about half their free throws.

6. (b) They both won All-Star Slam Dunk contests.
One of the great all-time slammers, Jordan won the
contest in both 1987 and 1988 at the NBA All-Star
weekend competitions. Carter won the title in 2000.

Game 20
Shooting Gallery

1. sky-hook
2. free throw
3. sky-hook
4. dunk
5. three-point line

6. field goal
7. one
8. overhand
9. player B
10. rebound

Game 21
Oddballs

1. (b) PPG. This is the abbreviation for "points per
   game"—you see it in players' statistics. MVP
   stands for "Most Valuable Player," DPY for
   "Defensive Player of the Year," and ROY for
   "Rookie of the Year," which are player awards.
2. (d) Loonie. It's the Canadian $1 coin. The other
   three are nicknames of players: "Zo" is Alonzo
   Mourning, "White Chocolate" is Jason Williams,

and "Penny" is the name Anfernee Hardaway goes by.

3. (c) Suns. The Suns is Phoenix's NBA team. The other three are women's teams in the WNBA.

4. (d) Bomb. A bomb is a shot made from a great distance. The other three are names for the ball.

5. (c) Player is sprayed with a water hose. This is the only item that is not a possible penalty for a violation or foul—however tempting it might be at times!

Game 22
Sign Language

(a) Pushing

(b) Illegal dribbling

(c) Traveling

(d) Three-point field goal attempt

(e) Three-point field goal successful

(f) Blocking

(g) 20-second timeout

(h) Holding

(i) Technical foul

Game 23
Play–by–Play

1. Blue passes the ball to White, who catches it on a jump and dunks it.
2. Green gets the rebound.
3. The Leopards make illegal moves against the Bears.
4. Red dribbles fast from one end of the court to the other.
5. Gray passes to an unguarded teammate.
6. Oops! Here is the announcer's mistake. If Navy shoots from 5 m (16 ft.) out, she's inside the three-point line. Her basket is worth only two points. (In the NBA, the top of the three-point arc is 6.7 m/22 ft. out from the net. Even in college games, it's 5.8 m/19 ft. from the basket.)

Game 24
All Mixed Up

1. jump shot
2. personal
3. Chicago Bulls
4. crossover
5. fast break
6. Olympic
7. substitutes
8. Boston Celtics
9. coach
10. flagrant

Game 25
Girls Got Game

1. (c) 1979. Ann Meyers tried out for the Indiana Pacers. She soon discovered she was too small to compete with guys 2 m (7 ft.) tall and built of solid muscle. However, her star-spangled career in college and on the U.S. women's national team earned her a place in the Basketball Hall of Fame.

2. (c) With few slam dunks or sky-hooks. Most women don't have the height and strength needed for those high-flying shots—although that may change.

3. (a) Precision and (b) Smart moves and plays. Women make up for their smaller size by perfecting the fundamental skills and plays.

4. (a) American women's professional leagues established in 1997. Since then, women have been able to play professionally in the United States.

5. (c) Six players. Today, women's teams, like men's teams, have five players.

6. (b) Europe, Asia, and South America. Many American players developed their pro skills there.

7. (a) Lisa Leslie and (b) Rebecca Lobo. Both were members of the Olympic team in Atlanta, whereas Cheryl Miller played on the winning team in the

Los Angeles Olympics in 1984.

8. (b) Can have jerseys worn outside the shorts. This is an option if the uniform is designed to be worn that way; however, the neatly tucked-in look is taking over. Since the 1999–2000 season, women's jerseys must be designed so that they can be worn tucked in.

Game 26
Alphabet Hoop

1. (b) field goals attempted
2. (a) field goals made
3. (c) free throws attempted
4. (a) free throws made
5. (b) points per game
6. (b) personal fouls
7. (c) offensive rebounds—rebounds grabbed after a missed shot by a teammate
8. (a) defensive rebounds—rebounds grabbed after a missed shot by the opposing team
9. (b) steals
10. (b) blocked shots
11. (b) three-point shots—shots made from behind the three-point line
12. (c) three-point shots attempted

Game 27
Word Jam

1. B.C.
2. Boston
3. cut
4. foul
5. from
6. goal
7. got
8. Heat
9. hot
10. L.A.
11. Magic
12. mates

13. no (No. 14 backwards)
14. on
15. out
16. rim
17. run
18. score
19. Shaq
20. sixth
21. Spurs
22. steal
23. Tim
24. time

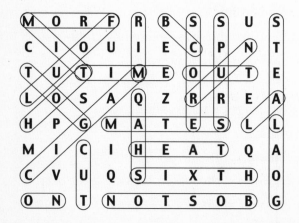

Game 28
Skill Drill

1. False. Players should learn to dribble well with either hand.
2. False. You should keep your eyes on what's going on around you.
3. True.
4. False. It's a tricky pass, since you can't see your target, though it's sometimes useful. Better practice a lot before trying it in a game.
5. False. Most passes are made with both hands.
6. False. Faking a pass can be an excellent move.
7. True.
8. False. The alley-oop pass is a difficult pass because it takes perfect timing. One player passes the ball in an easy arc to a teammate, who catches it on a jump and puts it in the basket.
9. False. You should hold the ball with your fingertips.
10. True.
11. False. You start standing sideways or with your back to the basket, then sweep your arm around and behind you.
12. False. A free throw is worth one point.
13. True.
14. True. A good rebounder blocks opponents from getting there first.
15. False. This counts as a regular field goal worth two points.